# Contents

**What is metal?**    **6**

**Where does metal come from?**    **8**

**Building with metal**    **10**

**Metal at home**    **12**

**Metal in the kitchen**    **14**

**Food and drink**    **16**

**Metal in transport**    **18**

**Metal in the garden**    **20**

**Beautiful metals**    **22**

**Other uses of metal**    **24**

**Recycling metal**    **26**

**Glossary**    **28**

**Index**    **30**

Words in **bold** are in the glossary.

# What is metal?

Metal is a **natural material**. There are many different types of metal. Most metal is hard.

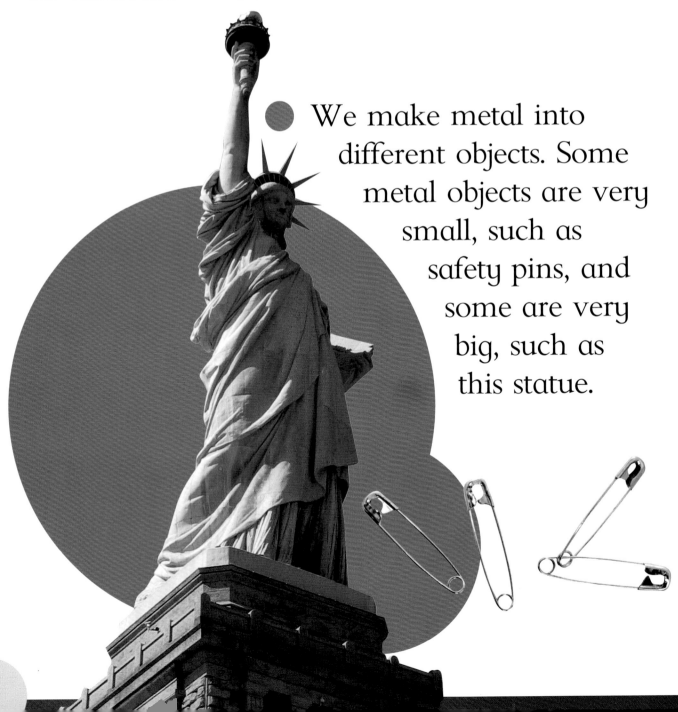

We make metal into different objects. Some metal objects are very small, such as safety pins, and some are very big, such as this statue.

# Metal

**Rita Storey**

W
FRANKLIN WATTS
LONDON•SYDNEY

First published in 2006 by
Franklin Watts
338 Euston Road
London NW1 3BH

Franklin Watts Australia
Hachette Children's Books
Level 17/207 Kent Street
Sydney NSW 2000

Art director: Jonathan Hair
Series designed and created for Franklin Watts by Painted Fish Ltd.
Designer: Rita Storey
Editor: Fiona Corbridge

Picture credits
Corbis/Duomo p. 23 (bottom), Corbis/Ted Spiegel p. 8, Corbis/Michael S. Yamashita
p. 27 (top), Corbis/Bo Zanders p. 9 (bottom); istockphoto.com p. 3,
p. 6, p. 7 (top), p. 7 (bottom), p. 9 (top), p. 10, p. 11, p. 12, p. 13, p. 14, p.
15 (middle and bottom), p. 17 (middle), p. 18, p. 19, p. 20, p. 21, p. 22, p. 25 (top),
p. 26, p. 27 (bottom); Tudor Photography p. 5, p. 7 (middle), p. 15 (top), p. 16,
p. 17 (top and bottom), p. 23 (top), p. 24, p. 25 (bottom).

Cover images: Tudor Photography, Banbury

ISBN 13: 978 0 7496 6453 4
Dewey classification: 669

A CIP catalogue record for this book is available from the British Library.

Printed in China

Franklin Watts is a division of Hachette Children's Books,
an Hachette Livre UK company.

Things made from metal can be very heavy, such as this truck. They can also be very light, like this drinks can.

Some metal is soft and we can bend it. Some metal is very strong. Parts of this aeroplane **engine** are made of very strong metal.

# Where does metal come from?

Metal is found inside rocks or in the ground. Rocks that have metal in them are called **ores**.

The place where we get ore out of the ground is called a mine.

To get ores out of the ground we use explosives or big drills like this one.

**Iron** is a metal that comes from iron ore. To get it, we heat iron ore in a very hot oven called a furnace. The metal melts and is collected.

We can find pieces of some metals, such as **gold**, in the Earth or in rivers. A lump of gold is called a nugget. This man is trying to find gold nuggets in a river.

nugget

*Metal keywords*

Ore
Mine
Iron
Gold
Nugget

# Building with metal

Metal is strong and can be made into all sorts of shapes. This makes it a good building material.

- We can heat iron until it becomes a **liquid**. Then we can pour it into a **mould**. The iron hardens when it cools and takes on the shape of the mould.

Metals can be mixed together to make a new metal called an **alloy**. Alloys are very strong.

Iron is mixed with other metals to make an alloy called **steel**. Steel is stronger than iron. It can be shaped in moulds to make the **frames** of buildings.

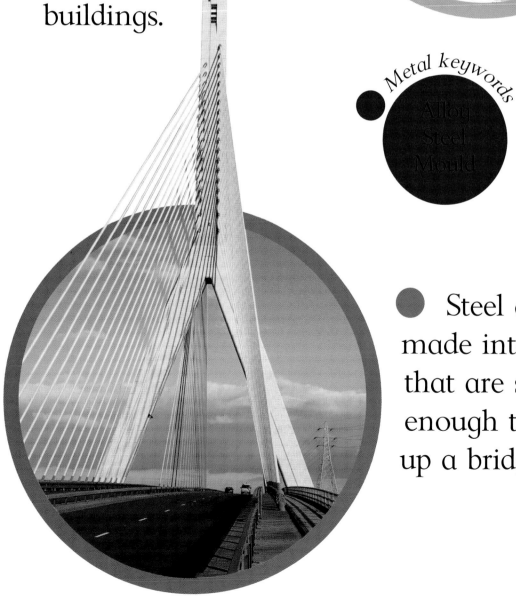

Metal keywords

Alloy
Steel
Mould

Steel can be made into ropes that are strong enough to hold up a bridge.

# Metal at home

We use metals for different jobs in our homes.

- **Copper** is a reddish-brown metal. It can be bent and shaped easily.

  Copper is used to make pipes that carry water to sinks and baths.

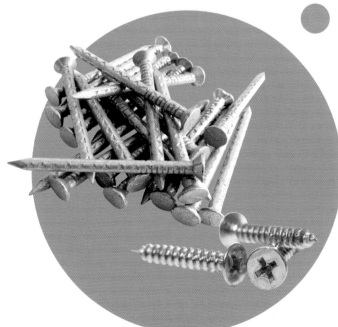

- Nails and screws are made of metal such as steel. They hold things together.

*Metal keywords*
Copper
Conducts
Brass
Zinc

Metal lets electricity **flow** through it - we say that it **conducts** electricity.

Copper **wires** carry electricity around our homes. Wires carrying electricity are covered in plastic. The plastic stops the electricity getting out of the wires.

**Brass** is a mixture of copper and **zinc**. It can be polished to make it shine. These taps are made of brass.

# Metal in the kitchen

Look around your kitchen.
How many metal objects
can you see?

Metal is used to make pans.
The metal lets the heat from
the cooker go through the pan
and heat up the food
inside. We say
that metal
conducts heat.

Copper and
**aluminium** are
good conductors
of heat.

Knives, forks, spoons and cooking tools are made from an alloy called **stainless steel**. It is shiny and easy to wash.

Metal can be made into a tube shape. Tubes are light and strong. They can be bent to make things like this stool.

*Metal keywords*

Shiny
Stainless steel
Aluminium

# Food and drink

Metal is used to make **packaging** for food and drink.

- Aluminium is a metal. It can be rolled into thin, bendy sheets. These are used to make some drinks cans.

- Foil is a very thin sheet of aluminium. We buy it on a roll to use in the kitchen. We can wrap food in foil before we cook it. It keeps steam in and stops the food drying out.

Foil containers are good for cooking food in. They can be heated up quickly.

Factories use foil for packaging food. It is **waterproof** and **airtight**, and keeps out light. These coffee beans will stay fresh for longer in foil wrapping.

*Metal keywords*

Cans
Foil
Waterproof
Airtight

Food is **sealed** in steel cans. This makes the food last for a long time.

# Metal in transport

Metal is used to make cars, bikes and aeroplanes because it is strong.

- Steel can be rolled into sheets and bent into different shapes. It is used to make cars.

- Air and water make iron and steel go **rusty**. This means that the metal turns a reddish colour and breaks up. Paint helps to stop metal rusting. On old cars, the paint may crack. Then the metal will rust.

Aeroplanes have to be strong, but they also need to be light so that they will fly.

Metal keywords

Rolled
Sheets
Rusty

Aluminium is light but not very strong. It is mixed with stronger metals to make an alloy that is used for aeroplanes.

The frame of this bicycle is made of aluminium alloy. It is very light but strong.

# Metal in the garden

Metal is useful for making tools and other things we use in the garden.

Iron and steel will rust if they are left outside. If steel is coated with zinc, it stops it rusting. This steel watering can has a zinc coating.

This ladder is made from aluminium so it is light and easy to carry.

This greenhouse has a frame made of an aluminium alloy, which does not rust. The greenhouse will last for a long time.

Iron can be hammered or bent into shapes like the ones on this gate.

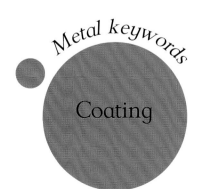

Metal keywords

Coating

# Beautiful metals

Metals can be shaped and moulded to make beautiful objects.

- Gold, **platinum** and **silver** are easy to shape and always stay shiny. This makes them good metals for making jewellery such as these bracelets.

● Gold has to be mixed with a harder metal before it can be used to make rings like these.

● Gold, silver and **bronze** are used to make **medals**. In lots of sports, a gold medal like this is the highest prize you can win.

*Metal keywords*

● Platinum
Silver
Bronze

# Other uses of metal

Metals are used to make things we use every day.

- Some paint is stored in metal cans. The cans are airtight and stop the paint drying out.

Shopping trolleys and baskets are often made of steel because it does not break.

Coins are made of metal because it is hard to break. They can be pressed into shape and stamped with a pattern.

Metal keywords

Coins

Keys

Metal is used to make keys. The metal will not bend or snap when you turn the key in the lock. These keys are made of brass and steel.

# Recycling metal

It takes millions of years for metal ores to form in the Earth. If we keep taking metal ores to use, they will run out one day.

● If we **recycle** metals, we do not need to take so much ore from the ground. It also means we do not need as many mines, which spoil large areas of the countryside. This area used to be a copper mine.

● Making new cans uses a lot of **energy**. Instead, we can make new cans from recycled old cans. This uses much less energy.

● Some materials pull iron and steel towards them. They are called **magnets**. It is easy to get iron and steel out of a pile of waste metals with a strong magnet. Then the metal can be melted down to make more steel objects.

*Metal keywords*

Recycling
Magnet

# Glossary

**Airtight** Keeps out the air.

**Alloy** A metal that is made by mixing two or more metals.

**Aluminium** A silvery-coloured metal. Mixed with other metals to make strong, lightweight objects.

**Brass** A mixture of zinc and copper.

**Bronze** A mixture of copper, tin and zinc.

**Conducts** Lets something pass from one place to another.

**Copper** A reddish-brown metal that does not rust.

**Energy** The power taken from fuel, which is used for light and heat and to move machinery.

**Engine** The part of a car or aeroplane that makes it move.

**Flow** Pass through.

**Frames** Pieces of metal joined together. Frames are used to help hold up parts of a building.

**Gold** A shiny yellow metal.

**Iron** A metal that is usually mixed with other metals to make steel.

**Liquid** A material such as water that flows.

**Magnets** Objects that pull iron or steel towards them.

**Medals** Flat pieces of metal given as a prize.

**Mould** A shape that liquid metal is poured into to make a different shape.

**Natural material** Comes from the Earth, plants or animals.

**Ores** Rocks that contain metal.

**Packaging** Something food and drinks are put in to keep them clean and safe.

**Plastic** A material made in factories from chemicals.

**Platinum** A silver-white metal used for jewellery.

**Recycle** Use a material again.

**Rusty** When metal is covered in rust - a reddish-coloured coating that makes the metal break up.

**Sealed** Closed very tightly.

**Silver** A shiny, greyish-white metal used to make jewellery and medals.

**Stainless steel** Steel that does not rust or stain.

**Steel** A very strong alloy of iron.

**Waterproof** Does not let water pass through.

**Wires** Long, thin pieces of metal.

**Zinc** A silvery-blue metal. It is used to cover steel to stop it rusting.

# Index

aeroplanes  18, 19
airtight  17, 24, 28
alloys  10, 11, 15, 19, 21, 28
aluminium  14, 16, 19, 20, 21, 28

bicycles  18, 19
brass  13, 25, 28
bronze  23, 28
building materials 10, 11, 21

cans  7, 16, 17, 24, 27
cars  18
coating  20
coins  25
conductors  13, 14, 28
cooking pans  14
copper  12, 13, 14, 28

electricity  13
energy  27, 28
engines  7, 28

foil  16, 17
frames  11, 19, 21, 28

furnaces  9

gold  9, 22, 23, 28

heat  14, 17

iron  9, 10, 11, 18, 20, 21, 27, 28

jewellery  22, 23

keys  25
knives, forks, spoons  15

liquid  10, 28

magnets  27, 29
medals  23, 29
mines  8, 26
moulds  10, 11, 29

nails  12
natural materials  6, 29
nuggets  9

ores  8, 9, 26, 29

packaging  16, 17, 29
pipes  12
plastic  13, 29
platinum  22, 29

recycling  26, 27, 29
ropes  11
rust  18, 20, 29

screws  12
sheets  16, 18
shopping trolleys 24
silver  22, 23, 29
stainless steel  15, 29
steel  11, 18, 20, 24, 27, 29

tools  15, 20
tubes  15

waterproof  17, 29
wires  13, 29

zinc  13, 20, 29